SIBO COOKBOOK

**MAIN COURSE – 80+ Recipes
designed to heal gastritis, intestinal
candida and other GUT health issues
(GERD & IBS effective approach)**

TABLE OF CONTENTS

- From a Declaration of Principles which was accepted and approved equally by a Committee of the American Bar Association and a Committee of Publishers and Associations.

The information herein is offered for informational purposes solely, and is universal as so. The presentation of the information is without contract or any type of guarantee assurance.

The trademarks that are used are without any consent, and the publication of the trademark is without permission or backing by the trademark owner. All trademarks and brands within this book are for clarifying purposes only and are the owned by the owners themselves, not affiliated with this document.

Introduction

SIBO recipes for family and personal enjoyment. You will love them for how easy it is to prepare them.

Serves: *1*

Prep Time: *10* minutes

Cook Time: *8* hours

Total Time: *8* hours and 10 minutes

INGREDIENTS

- 1/3 cup pumpkin puree
- 1/3 cup coconut milk
- 1 tablespoon flour
- 1 tablespoon collagen hydrolysate
- ½ tablespoon cinnamon
- ¼ tablespoon ginger
- 1/8 tablespoon gloves

DIRECTIONS

1. In a bawl add the ingredients, pumpkin puree, milk, cinnamon, ginger and so on and stir to mix thoroughly
2. Cover the bowl and put in the refrigerator
3. In the morning enjoy your breakfast

Serves: *1*

Prep Time: *5*   minutes

Cook Time: *15*   minutes

Total Time: *20*   minutes

INGREDIENTS

- 1 slice of bacon
- 3-4 oz. ground beef
- 1 oz. chicken liver
- chopped handful of chopped veggies

DIRECTIONS

1. In a pan cook the bacon on low heat
2. Meanwhile cook the ground beef, when done mix with the chicken liver
3. Add chopped veggies in the bacon
4. Strain off excess grease from ground beef mixture
5. Add baby greens and when ready serve

Serves: *1*

Prep Time: *5*   minutes

Cook Time: *10*   minutes

Total Time: *15*   minutes

INGREDIENTS

- 1 cup raw cashews
- ½ cups dehydrated strawberries
- 1 ½ tablespoons cinnamon
- ½ teaspoons sea salt

DIRECTIONS

1. Use a food processor and pulse the dehydrated fruits into small pieces, pour them into a bowl and set aside
2. Also add cashews to food processor and blend for a couple of minutes, keep going until it gets creamy
3. Once it gets creamy add the cinnamon and strawberries and blend for another 2-3 minutes
4. Let them mix completely and let the mixture cool down for a couple of hours
5. Store in the fridge and serve when you want

Serves: 2

Prep Time: *10*   minutes

Cook Time: *10*   minutes

Total Time: *20*   minutes

INGREDIENTS

- 6 eggs
- 1 jalapeno
- ¼ cups white onion
- ¼ cups mushroom
- 1 cup almond milk
- 1 tablespoon butter
- salt
- pepper

DIRECTIONS

1. Take a skillet and add butter to melt over low heat
2. When butter melts add onion, mushroom and jalapeno, sauté for 5 minutes
3. In a bowl crack the eggs and add pepper and almond milk and whisk well

4. Pour the mixture into a skillet and cook on low heat until the eggs are fully cooked

5. Serve with bacon when is ready

MORNING MUFFINS

Serves: **1**

Prep Time: **5**   minutes

Cook Time: **10**   minutes

Total Time: **15**   minutes

INGREDIENTS

- 1 banana
- ½ cups nut butter
- 1 tablespoons cinnamon
- 2 teaspoons vanilla
- 1 tablespoon honey
- ¼ teaspoon baking soda

DIRECTIONS

1. Preheat the oven to 420 F and put a muffin tin inside of it

2. Mix all the ingredients in a food processor and blend until is well done

3. Into the muffin tin pour the mixture and bake for 10-12 minutes

4. Remove from the oven and let it cool

SWEET POTATO HASH

Serves: 2

Prep Time: *10*   minutes

Cook Time: *20*   minutes

Total Time: *30*   minutes

INGREDIENTS

- 2 sweet potatoes
- 1 bell pepper
- 1 large red onion

- ¼ cup green onion
- 2 garlic cloves
- 3 tablespoons olive oil
- 2 teaspoons pepper
- ¼ teaspoons sea salt

DIRECTIONS

1. Take a skillet and heat olive oil over low heat
2. Add sweet potatoes and cook for about 5-10 minutes
3. When sweet potatoes start to get a brown color add peeper, green onion, red onion, salt, garlic and sauté for the next 12-15 minutes
4. Stir the mixture until, not to burn or stick in the skillet
5. Cook until the mixture is tender, about 5-10 minutes

Serves: **1**
Prep Time: **5**   minutes

Cook Time: **10**   minutes

Total Time: **15**   minutes

INGREDIENTS

- 1 cup sweet potato
- ½ pounds turkey chorizo
- 6 eggs
- ½ cups white onion
- ¼ cups coconut milk
- 2 tablespoons olive oil
- 1 tablespoon rosemary
- 1 teaspoon pepper
- ¼ teaspoon sea salt

DIRECTIONS

1. Take a skillet and heat oil over low heat
2. In a skillet place chorizo and onion, cook for 3-4 minutes

3. When chorizo is cooked add sweet potato and cook for 5-10 minutes, add rosemary and stir

4. In a bowl add eggs, milk and whisk

5. Pour the eggs over the mixture, lower the heat and cook slowly until is cooked completely

6. Flip the frittata on both sides and cook for another 4-5 minutes, move to a place and serve

HAM AND BROCCOLI EGG BREAFAST

Serves: *1*

Prep Time: *5* minutes

Cook Time: *10* minutes

Total Time: *15* minutes

INGREDIENTS

- 12 eggs
- 6 slices of ham
- 12 broccoli florets
- 1 ounce cheddar cheese
- 1 dash salt
- 1 dash pepper

DIRECTIONS

1. Preheat the oven to 350 F
2. Prepare muffin tin by lining with cups
3. Take ham and put in each cup with broccoli floret
4. In a bowl mix egg, salt and pepper
5. Pour the eggs into each cup
6. Cook for 15-20 minutes
7. Remove from the oven and let them cool

EGG & TURKEY STACK

Serves: **1**

Prep Time: **10** minutes

Cook Time: **10** minutes

Total Time: **20** minutes

INGREDIENTS

- 2 turkey lunchmeat
- 2 egg

- 1 slice of organic cheese
- 1 tablespoons Giardiniera

DIRECTIONS

1. Take a bowl add eggs and whisk
2. Pile the turkey on a plate
3. When the eggs are ready place them over the turkey
4. Add cheese on top and let sit for 1-2 minutes
5. Remove bowl and top with Giardiniera and serve

HONEY CANDIED BACON

Serves: *1*
Prep Time: *5*   minutes

Cook Time: *10*   minutes

Total Time: *15*   minutes

INGREDIENTS

- 1-pound bacon

- 4 tablespoons honey
- 1 tablespoon water
- 1 tablespoon olive oil

DIRECTIONS

1. Preheat oven to 325 F and place a pan in it
2. Add olive oil and lay your bacon in side by side and cook for 10-15 minutes
3. Add honey over the bacon, carefully not to burn it
4. Remove bacon from the oven and drain grease
5. If you consider necessary, bake for another 5-10 minutes

WAFFLES WITH HONEY PEACH SYRUP

Serves: **2**
Prep Time: **10** minutes

Cook Time: **10** minutes

Total Time: **20** minutes

INGREDIENTS

Waffles ingredients

- 3 eggs
- ¾ cup raw cashews
- ¼ cups raw pecans
- 1/3 cups almond milk
- 3 tablespoons coconut oil
- 3 tablespoons honey
- ¼ cup coconut flour
- ¾ teaspoons baking soda
- ¼ teaspoons sea salt

PEACH HONEY SYRUP

- 3 peaches
- 3 tablespoons
- ¼ cup honey
- ¼ cups water
- 1 tablespoons cinnamon
- 1/8 tablespoons sea salt

DIRECTIONS

Waffles Directions

1. Preheat a pan or a waffle iron
2. Mix together milk, honey nuts and oil

3. When first ingredients are mixed add flour, salt and baking soda

4. Pour the mixture in the pan or in the waffle iron

5. Enjoy when ready!

Peach honey Syrup Directions

1. In a skillet melt palm over low heat

2. Add peaches and sauté for 5-10 minutes

3. Add water and salt and simmer for 5 minutes

4. Add cinnamon and honey and stir for 5-10 minutes

5. Remove from heat and let it cool for 5-10 minutes

FILLING BACON AND LENTIL SOUP

Serves: **4**

Prep Time: **10**   minutes

Cook Time: **25**   minutes

Total Time: **35**   minutes

INGREDIENTS

- 1 ½ cups chopped leek
- ¾ lbs bacon
- 1 ½ cups diced carrots
- 1 large chopped parsley
- 1 cup thyme leaves
- 1 cup brown lentils
- 3 cups purple kale
- 6-8 cups marrow bone broth
- 1 tablespoon olive oil
- salt

DIRECTIONS

1. Chop the bacon, place it in a soup pot and add olive oil

2. Place the pot over high heat and stir frequently

3. Add chopped leek, parsley, kale, carrots and lower the heat

4. Cook for 5-10 minutes and add lentils, 6 cups of broth and thyme

5. Simmer and cook for 15-20 minutes

6. Remove the bundle of thyme and add the rest of the broth

ELK STEW

Serves: 2

Prep Time: **20**   minutes

Cook Time: **25**   minutes

Total Time: **45**   minutes

INGREDIENTS

- 1 lb elk roast or steak
- 1tablespoon butter
- 3 cups bone

- 1 cup chopped carrots
- 2 cups chopped zucchini
- 1 cup green cabbage
- 1cup sliced leek
- 8 leaves sage minced
- 10 dried juniper berries
- 2 stems rosemary
- salt

DIRECTIONS

1. Mince the sage, remove the leaves from the rosemary and set aside
2. Take the elk and slice it, in a skillet melt butter
3. Take the elk and place it in the pan, after 1-2 minutes flip each piece over
4. When the meat is cooked move it to an instant pot, fill with broth and add half of the minced herbs, leek and salt
5. Add vegetables and the remaining broth, remove from the heat and let it cool

Serves: *1*

Prep Time: *10*   minutes

Cook Time: *10*   minutes

Total Time: *20*   minutes

INGREDIENTS

- ½ cup roasted chicken
- 1 orange
- ¼ cup nuts
- 1 cup chopped lettuce
- 1 tablespoon sliced scallions
- ½ lemon
- ¼ cup apple vinegar
- ½ tablespoon honey
- salt

DIRECTIONS

1. In a bowl place the lettuce and decorate with the chicken, scallions, orange and nuts
2. Juice the lemon in a jar and add apple vinegar, oil, salt and honey

Serves: **1**

Prep Time: **10**   minutes

Cook Time: **45**   minutes

Total Time: **55**   minutes

INGREDIENTS

- 1 quart homemade tomato sauce
- 1 can coconut milk
- 2 tablespoons minced fresh basil
- 1 tablespoons honey
- salt
- 1 cup cheese

DIRECTIONS

1. In a soup pot pour coconut milk and heat over high heat, add tomato sauce, honey, basil and salt
2. Simmer for 10-15 minutes
3. Preheat the oven to 425 F
4. Place a piece of parchment paper onto a baking sheet
5. Place small piles of cheese on the baking sheet, the cheese will melt down and spread

6. Place it in the oven for 5-10 minutes

7. Remove the crisps from the oven onto a plate and let it cool for 1-2 minutes

ROAST CHICKEN

Serves: **1**

Prep Time: **10** minutes

Cook Time: **65** minutes

Total Time: **75** minutes

INGREDIENTS

- 1 raw chicken
- 1 tablespoon melted butter
- 1 tablespoon dried herbs
- salt

DIRECTIONS

1. Preheat the oven to 400 F

2. In a pan place the raw chicken and spread olive oil on the chicken, also add salt and herbs

3. Place the chicken in the oven for 55-65 minutes

SAUSAGE

Serves: *1*

Prep Time: *10*   minutes

Cook Time: *15*   minutes

Total Time: *25*   minutes

INGREDIENTS

- 1 pound ground pork
- 2 pounds ground beef
- 3 tablespoons minced sage
- 2 tablespoons fresh minced thyme
- 1 tablespoons rosemary
- 2 tablespoons honey
- 1 tablespoon salt
- pepper

DIRECTIONS

1. In a bowl place the ground meat
2. Mix the pepper, honey, salt, rosemary, thyme and sage in the same bowl with the meat and mix all of them together
3. Form into disks and cook in a skillet on medium heat

CHERRY TOMATO CHICHKEN

Serves: 2

Prep Time: *10*   minutes

Cook Time: *35*   minutes

Total Time: *45*   minutes

INGREDIENTS

- 4 chicken things
- 1 tablespoon olive oil
- 20 cherry tomatoes
- ¼ cup chopped fennel
- ¼ cup chopped celery

- ¼ chopped red bell pepper
- 1 tablespoon dried marjoram
- wine vinegar
-

DIRECTIONS

1. Sauté all the ingredients in olive oil and them put the veggies aside
2. Cook the chicken pieces and until gold-brown on both sides and add vinegar, marjoram and chicken broth
3. In your skillet cook on low heath for 30-35 minutes until is don
4. Sprinkle with parsley and serve!

Serves: *1*

Prep Time: *10*   minutes

Cook Time: **25**   minutes

Total Time: **35**   minutes

INGREDIENTS

- 8 cups chicken broth
- 2 chicken breasts
- 4 baby bok choy (chopped)
- ½ piece ginger
- 1 tablespoon coconut Aminos
- 2 eggs

DIRECTIONS

1. In a sauce pan boil he chicken, slice the chicken breasts and add in the sauce pan to boil, stir for 4-5 minutes

2. While boiling add bok choy and stir frequently for 4-5 minutes

3. Whisk the eggs, stir until they are cooked through

4. Add ladle, scalliona and coconut aminos into bowls for serving

Serves: *4*

Prep Time: *10*   minutes

Cook Time: *15*   minutes

Total Time: *25*   minutes

INGREDIENTS

- 1-pound ground beef
- 1 egg
- 2 tablespoons fresh ginger
- ½ tablespoon cinnamon
- ¼ tablespoon cloves
- ¼ cup chopped cilantro
- ¼ cup chopped mint
- salt

DIRECTIONS

1. Combine all the ingredients together and when ready roll the meat onto skewers
2. Cook grilled on your barbeque for 10-15 o each side
3. Remove, let it cool for 1-2 minutes and serve

Serves: **2**

Prep Time: **10** minutes

Cook Time: **60** minutes

Total Time: **70** minutes

INGREDIENTS

- 6 springs rosemary
- 4 left whole zest and juice of 1 lime
- 3 tablespoons olive oil
- 1 tablespoon honey
- ½ tablespoons salt
- black pepper

DIRECTIONS

1. The the rosemary, lime juice, oil, honey salt and the rest of the ingredients and mix in to your roasting pan
2. Lay your chicken into the pan and turn repeatedly until is fully coated with the marinade
3. Cover the chicken with a tent of aluminum for 40-45 minutes
4. Remove the foil and roast for another 15-20 minutes

Serves: *2*

Prep Time: *10*   minutes

Cook Time: *65*   minutes

Total Time: *75*   minutes

INGREDIENTS

- 2 pounds beef
- ½ cup coconut flour
- ½ tablespoon rubbed thyme
- ½ tablespoons salt
- ½ tablespoon cinnamon
- ¼ tablespoon black pepper
- 1 slice of bacon
- 3 slices celery root
- 3 sliced red pepper
- ¼ cup olive oil
- 5 chopped tomatoes
- 2 scallions
- 1/3 cup red wine
- oregano

DIRECTIONS

1. Heat a frying pan over medium heat

2. Add bacon, red pepper and celery and cook until vegetables are soft

3. In a bowl add coconut flour, cinnamon, thyme and pepper, mix well and add each piece of beef

4. Lay each piece of beef flat and pound lightly with a meat mallet

5. Remove and reserve the softened vegetables and bacon from the pan

6. Add olive oil and increase the heat

7. Lay the floured beef into the bacon oil and cook on both sides

8. When the beef is ready add chopped tomatoes and cook for 4-5 minutes

9. Add bacon, vegetables, scallion and wine in the pan, also add water to prevent the sauce from sticking, lower the heat and simmer for at least 1 hour

Serves: **1**

Prep Time: **10** minutes

Cook Time: **10** minutes

Total Time: **20** minutes

INGREDIENTS

- 2 medium zucchini
- juice of ½ lemon
- juice of ½ lime
- ½ tablespoon mustard
- ½ tablespoon honey
- ½ cup olive oil
- salt
- 1 tablespoon thyme
- ½ cup parmesan cheese

DIRECTIONS

1. In a Pyrex measuring cup blend honey, mustard, lemon juice, lime juice and olive oil
2. Add salt if necessary

3. Combine the mixture in a bowl with zucchini, thyme and parmesan and toss well

SUMMER SHISH KEBABS

Serves: *1*
Prep Time: *20*   minutes

Cook Time: *25*   minutes

Total Time: *45*   minutes

INGREDIENTS

- 2 chicken breasts
- 1 small eggplant
- 1 medium zucchini
- 1 red pepper

Barbeque Marinade
- 3 tablespoon tomato paste
- ½ tablespoon cumin
- ½ tablespoon coriander
- ½ tablespoon oregano
- ¼ tablespoon cinnamon

-   2 tablespoons cider vinegar

-   1 tablespoon coconut aminos

-   1 tablespoon mustard

DIRECTIONS

1. Mix the marinade ingredients in a bowl

2. Add to the mixture the chicken breast and stir to coat all the pieces

3. Cut the zucchini, eggplant and red pepper

4. Skewer the chicken and vegetables

5. Place the shish kebabs into the rill and cook, turn on each side every 4-5 minutes until they are equally grilled

6. Remove from the grill when ready, let it cool for 1-2 minutes and serve!

Serves: **4**

Prep Time: **10**   minutes

Cook Time: **60**   minutes

Total Time: **70**   minutes

INGREDIENTS

- 1 pound beef ribs
- 1 tablespoon grated
- 3 tablespoons coconut Aminos
- juice fro ½ lime
- juice from ½ orange
- ½ tablespoons coriander
- ½ tablespoons turmeric
- ¼ black pepper

DIRECTIONS

1. In a bowl blend all the marinade ingredients together
2. Dredge each rib in the marinade and allow to marinate for 45-60 minutes
3. Grill the ribs until done, 4-5 minutes per each side on low-medium hea

Serves: *1*

Prep Time: *10* minutes

Cook Time: *15* minutes

Total Time: *25* minutes

INGREDIENTS

- 2 grilled chicken breasts
- 1 papaya
- 5 red peppers
- 1 tablespoon coconut oil
- 2 tablespoons honey
- 4 cups arugula
- 2 tablespoons flaked coconut
- 2 tablespoons macadamia nuts
- black pepper

DIRECTIONS

1. Place a pan over medium heat, sauté peppers in coconut oil
2. When the peppers are soft add diced papaya, continue to cook for a couple of more minutes

3. Add honey and chicken tossing the pan to coat the ingredients

4. Cook everything for 4-5 minutes

5. Add the arugula, tossing the pan to coat

6. Turn the hash into a serving plate

STRAWBERRY CHICKEN WITH SPINACH

Serves: 2

Prep Time: **10**   minutes

Cook Time: **15**   minutes

Total Time: **25**   minutes

INGREDIENTS

- 3 boneless chicken thighs
- 1 tablespoon walnut oil
- 6 strawberries
- 2 tablespoons apple vinegar
- 1 tablespoon honey
- 2 tablespoons walnuts

- 1 plastic container of spinach leaves
- ¼ cup water

DIRECTIONS

1. In a pan heat walnut oil over medium heat, add sauté the chicken thighs and cook for 4-5 minutes each side
2. Remove the chicken when ready and add vinegar, honey, strawberries, and walnuts to the pan
3. Cook on low heat
4. Cut chicken and add back to the pan and turn each piece to coat for 4-5 minutes
5. Add the spinach leaves and water, stir for 4-5 minutes
6. Place the saute onto two plates, top with sauced chicken and serve

Serves: 2

Prep Time: **20**   minutes

Cook Time: **35**   minutes

Total Time: **55**   minutes

INGREDIENTS

- 1 halibut fillet
- ¾ cup cherry tomatoes
- juice of ½ lime
- 1 tablespoon minced cilantro stems
- salt

DIRECTIONS

1. Cook the halibut on the grill
2. It will take roughly 5-10 minutes to cook a fillet sized
3. Combine all the ingredients in a bowl
4. Add the salsa to the pan around he fish and let the salsa warm for 2-3 minutes
5. Scoop the warmed salsa on top of the fish to soak in during the last minutes of cooking
6. Serve it and top with fresh cilantro leaves

Serves: *4*

Prep Time: *10*   minutes

Cook Time: *35*   minutes

Total Time: *45*   minutes

INGREDIENTS

-   8 boneless chicken thighs
-   olive oil
-   1/3 cup coconut four
-   1 tablespoon cinnamon
-   1 tablespoon dried ginger
-   ½ tablespoon turmeric
-   ½ tablespoon salt
-   ¼ tablespoon black pepper
-   1-inch piece of fresh ginger
-   1/3 cup dried papaya
-   ½ tablespoon sumac
-   2 tablespoon honey
-   2 cinnamon sticks
-   1 cup chicken broth
-   1 12 ounce can of diced tomatoes

- rosemary (as needed)

DIRECTIONS

1. In a bowl combine coconut flour, ginger, cinnamon, salt, turmeric and pepper until well mixed
2. In a frying pan our olive oil to cover the bottom of the pan over medium heat
3. Toss each chicken piece in coconut flour and cook it in the skillet for 5-10 minutes per side
4. As the chicken is browning strip the leaves leaves of rosemary and minced them
5. When the chicken is golden/brown remove from the pan and set aside

Serves: *3*

Prep Time: *20*   minutes

Cook Time: *25*   minutes

Total Time: *45*   minutes

INGREDIENTS

- 3 medium rutabagas
- 3 tablespoons butter
- 1 wedge parmesan cheese
- 4-5 springs of chives
- 1-2 cups of chicken broth
- fresh nutmeg

DIRECTIONS

1. Preheat the oven to 325 F
2. In a saucepan add sliced rutabagas with with water and boil them
3. Simmer until tender and add 1 tablespoon of butter to coat
4. Remove rutabagas and drain well
5. Place a payer of rutabagas on the bottom of your dish

6. Sprinkle cheese over the top, pepper and salt

7. Pour your liquid intro a casserole, grate fresh nutmeg over the finished top and cover with a foil

8. Bake for 45-60 minutes until cheese is melted

MEAT LOAF

Serves: **4**

Prep Time: **20**   minutes

Cook Time: **70**   minutes

Total Time: **90**   minutes

INGREDIENTS

- 1-pound beef
- ½ pound fresh pork
- ½ pound fresh turkey
- 1 cup mashed rutabaga
- ½ cup aged parmesan
- 1 egg
- 2 tablespoons tomato paste

- ½ tablespoons dried thyme
- ¼ tablespoons marjoram
- ½ tablespoons salt
- ½ tablespoon pepper
- 2 strips bacon

DIRECTIONS

1. Blend all the ingredients together and form into a loaf
2. Cut and lay strips of bacon evenly
3. Bake for 60 minutes until meat is ready
4. Turn the oven to the broil and cook for another 5-10 minutes
5. Remove and let it rest for 5-10 minutes

Serves: **2**

Prep Time: **10**   minutes

Cook Time: **25**   minutes

Total Time: **35**   minutes

INGREDIENTS

- 1 10 ounce package spinach leaves
- 1 large boneless chicken breast
- 2 teaspoons coconut oil
- 1tablespoon coconut aminos
- 1 teaspoon paprika
- 1 cup coconut milk
- 1tablespoon coconut flour
- 1tablespoon water
- 2 tablespoons lime juice

DIRECTIONS

1. Set steamer basket in a large pot and add water
2. Bring water to a boil and layer ¼ of the spinach in basket
3. Remove spinach to drain and place it on a plate

4. In a saucepan bring 8 cups of water to a boil over medium heat

5. Add chicken to the saucepan and lower the heat

6. Let the chicken stand in the boiled water

7. In a saucepan heat oil over low heat and add coconut aminos, peanut butter, paprika and fish sauce

8. Stir in coconut milk until well blended, reduce the heat and cook for another 4-5 minutes

9. To assemble everything drain the chicken, stir into hot peanut sauce and pour sauced chicken mixture over spinach

BUTTERNUT SQUASH SOUP

Serves: 2

Prep Time: 10   minutes

Cook Time: 55   minutes

Total Time: 65   minutes

INGREDIENTS

- 1 heaping tablespoons coconut oil
- ¼ tablespoons ginger

- 2 6" stalks of lemon grass
- 4 kaffir lime leaves
- 1 large butternut squash
- 1 cup home-made chicken broth
- 2 cans coconut milk
- salt

DIRECTIONS

1. In a pot add kaffir, lemon grass, ginger and coconut oil over low heat
2. Cook until softened for about 20 minutes
3. Add butternut squash cubes and stir until cubes are coted
4. Stir in chicken broth and cover with a lid and cook until squash is tender for 30 minutes
5. Add the coconut milk and blend
6. Taste and adjust with salt and pepper

Serves: **1**

Prep Time: **10**   minutes

Cook Time: **20**   minutes

Total Time: **30**   minutes

INGREDIENTS

- 1 salmon filet
- 2 tablespoons coconut oil
- ½ cup blueberries
- juice from ½ orange
- salt
- black pepper
- ¼ tablespoons nutmeg

DIRECTIONS

1. In a pan combine all the ingredients over low heat and stir frequently
2. When the blueberries are melted lower the heat until the salmon is done
3. In a pan move the salmon fillet and pour coconut oil

4. When it starts to have a golden color flit the salmon and continue cooking for 5-10 minutes

5. Remove and serve with butter-sautéed green beans

CARROT RED PEPPER SOUP

Serves: **1**

Prep Time: **10**   minutes

Cook Time: **70**   minutes

Total Time: **80**   minutes

INGREDIENTS

- Coconut oil
- 1 knob grated ginger
- 3 sage leaves
- 1 tablespoons curry powder
- ½ tablespoon cumin seeds
- ½ tablespoon cardamom
- ½ tablespoons coriander
- 1 red pepper
- 10 sliced carrots

- ½ tablespoons salt
- ¼ tablespoons white pepper

DIRECTIONS

1. In a pot add sage, spices, coconut oil, sauté ginger, red pepper, salt and carrot slices
2. Stir to coat and cook on low heat for 20 minutes
3. Add water to cover the vegetables and simmer for 50-60 minutes until carrots are tender
4. Remove from the heat and serve

HALIBUT WITH STRABERRY SAUCE

Serves: 2

Prep Time: 20   minutes

Cook Time: 25   minutes

Total Time: 45   minutes

INGREDIENTS

- 8 strawberries chopped fine
- juice from ½ orange

- ½ tablespoons honey
- salt
- 1 tablespoons mint

DIRECTIONS

1. Mix all the ingredients in a sauce pan over low heat and stir frequently while cooking
2. When the strawberries are melted turn off the heat
3. Pan-fry the halibut fillet in coconut oil, flip the fish on the other side and cook for 5-10 minutes
4. When ready remove from heat and place halibut on top of the greens, top with strawberry sauce and serve

BARBEQUE RIBS

Serves: 4
Prep Time: 10   minutes

Cook Time: 140   minutes

Total Time: 150   minutes

INGREDIENTS

- 1 rack of baby back pork
- 1 tablespoon paprika
- ½ tablespoon mustard
- ¼ tablespoon powdered thyme
- ¼ tablespoons rubbed sage
- 1 tablespoon salt
- 1 tablespoon white pepper

Marinate

- 2/3 cup tomato paste
- 2 tablespoons coconut aminos
- 1 tablespoons honey
- juice of ½ orange
- 1 tablespoons apple vinegar

DIRECTIONS

1. Combine the ingredients and add the pork ribs, place the ribs onto a large pan and cover the ribs with a foil
2. Refrigerate for at least 5 hours
3. Preheat oven to 250 F and place the ribs and bake for 2 hours
4. Combine marinade ingredients and season with salt
5. Remove the foil and baste the ribs with the marinade
6. Bake for another 20 minutes

Serves: *2*

Prep Time: *10*   minutes

Cook Time: *25*   minutes

Total Time: *35*   minutes

INGREDIENTS
- 1 cup shredded pork
- ½ red pepper
- 2 small zucchini
- 2 bok choy
- ¼ cup minted basil
- 1/8 cup Mint

Marinade

- 4 tablespoons fish sauce
- 4 tablespoons coconut aminos
- 2 tablespoons squeezed lime juice

DIRECTIONS

1. Mix the marinade and pour half the marinade over the cooked meat

2. In a wok add coconut oil, sauté, carrots and ginger over medium heat

3. Add zucchini and red pepper to the wok and continue to cook

4. Remove everything from the pan, add meat and cook for 4-5 minutes

5. Add bok choy and herbs and cook for 2-3 minutes

INDIAN BEEF

Serves: **2**

Prep Time: **10** minutes

Cook Time: **20** minutes

Total Time: **30** minutes

INGREDIENTS

- ¼ cup oil
- 1 ½ tablespoons cumin seeds
- 3 lbs ground hamburger
- 4 tablespoons fresh ginger
- 2 packages spinach
- 1 8 ounce diced tomatoes

- 1 tablespoon tomato paste
- 2 tablespoon ground turmeric
- 2 tablespoons curry powder
- 1 tablespoon ground cumin
- 1 tablespoons cinnamon
- 1/8 ground cloves
- 1 tablespoon garam masala
- ½ tablespoon salt
- ½ tablespoon black pepper
- 4 tablespoons chopped cilantro

DIRECTIONS

1. In a pot heat oil over medium heat cook for another 4-5 minutes and cumin seeds
2. Add meat and stir frequently, cook for another 5 minutes and add spinach
3. Add turmeric, tomato paste, curry, tomatoes and minced stems of cilantro, cook for another 10-15 minutes
4. Stir in cinnamon, cloves, cumin, salt, garam masala and cook for 4-5 minutes

Serves: *1*

Prep Time: *10*   minutes

Cook Time: *25*   minutes

Total Time: *35*   minutes

INGREDIENTS

- 2 jars of canned tomatoes
- 2 tablespoons fresh oregano
- 1 tablespoon ground cinnamon
- ¼ cup red wine
- 4 large eggplants
- salt
- 4 cups of parmesan cheese

DIRECTIONS

1. For tomato sauce add oregano, red wine, cinnamon, tomatoes and cook over low heat in a pot
2. Cook for 2-3 hours and simmer
3. Trim off the eggplants and arrange on a salted chopping mat and let the eggplant sit for 10-15 minutes

4. Heat a pan to medium, fry the slices on both sides for 5-10 minutes

5. Remove on a plate and let them cool

6. Preheat oven to 325 F

7. Assemble the eggplant parmesan and add tomato sauce, top sprinkle parmesan cheese over the sauced slices

8. Bake for 50-60 minutes until the cheese is melted, remove and serve

COLLARD GREENS WITH BACON AND TOMATO

Serves: *1*

Prep Time: *5*   minutes

Cook Time: *15*   minutes

Total Time: *20*   minutes

INGREDIENTS

- 1 bunch collard greens
- 1 tomato
- 4 strips bacon
- ½ lemon
- 1tablespoon honey
- ½ tablespoon salt
- 1/8 tablespoon black pepper
- red pepper
- parmesan cheese

DIRECTIONS

1. In a skillet cook bacon until crispy
2. Chop the bacon into small pieces and set aside

3. Keep bacon grease and sauté tomatoes until softened 5-10 minutes

4. Slice collard greens and stir them into tomato grease

5. Keep stirring until greens are coated and begin to soften

6. Add lemon juice, salt, honey and stir

7. Turn off heat, pour the excess juices and let it cool

8. Serve with parmesan

SESAME CUMIN ZUCCHINI

Serves: *1*

Prep Time: 5   minutes

Cook Time: **15**   minutes

Total Time: **20**   minutes

INGREDIENTS

- 3 zucchini
- 3 tablespoons garlic sesame oil
- ½ tablespoons salt
- 1 ½ tablespoon cumin

- ¼ tablespoon paprika
- ¼ tablespoon coriander
- ¼ lemon

DIRECTIONS

1. Cut zucchini in half
2. In a skillet add the zucchini over medium heat
3. Add garlic sesame oil and all the spices
4. Let zucchini brown on each side and squeeze lemon overtop
5. Remove from the skillet and serve

MOROCCAN EGGPLANT

Serves: **4**

Prep Time: **10**   minutes

Cook Time: **45**   minutes

Total Time: **55**   minutes

INGREDIENTS

- 1 eggplant
- 1 tomato-chopped
- ½ jalapeno minced
- 2 tablespoons garlic with sesame oil
- ½ lemon
- ½ tablespoon lemon juiced
- ¾ tablespoon salt
- 1/8 tablespoon black pepper
- ¾ tablespoon cumin
- ¼ tablespoon paprika
- ½ cup cilantro chopped

DIRECTIONS

1. Boil the eggplant for 20-25 minutes and drain water when ready
2. In a skillet add garlic sesame oil over medium heat and also add minced jalapeno
3. Add chopped tomatoes, eggplant, lemon rind and lemon juice
4. Let eggplant sauté until the water has cooked away, 20-25 minutes
5. Remove from heat and let it cool and serve!

Serves: *4*

Prep Time: *10*   minutes

Cook Time: *65*   minutes

Total Time: *75*   minutes

INGREDIENTS

- 1 lb green beans
- 1 cup chopped tomatoes
- 1 tablespoon lemon juice
- ½ tablespoon salt
- 1/8 tablespoons black pepper
- 2 tablespoons garlic oil
- 1/8 tablespoons chili flakes
- 2 tablespoons chopped basil

DIRECTIONS

1. In a skillet add olive oil over medium heat
2. Add the green beans into skillet and add tomato and salt

3. Cook on medium heat until tomatoes and beans are soft for 30-40 minutes, meanwhile add the rest of the ingrediens

4. Uncover and let juice cook for 30-40 minutes

5. Turn off heat, let it cool and serve

GARLIC SESAME BABY BOK CHOY

Serves: **4**

Prep Time: **10**   minutes

Cook Time: **15**   minutes

Total Time: **25**   minutes

INGREDIENTS

- 3 bok choy
- 2 tablespoons garlic sesame oil
- ¼ cup sesame seeds
- ½ tablespoons fish sauce
- 2 tablespoons coconut aminos

DIRECTIONS

1. Cover with 2 tablespoons of sesame oil a couple of cloves of garlic

2. Slice the baby choy and set aside

3. In a skillet add 2 tablespoons of garlic sesame oil over medium heat and et saute for 1-2 minutes

4. Add chopped bok choy, fish and coconut aminos and mix well

5. Remove from heat, let it cool and serve!

SIBO FRIES

Serves: **4**

Prep Time: **10**   minutes

Cook Time: **65**   minutes

Total Time: **75**   minutes

INGREDIENTS

- 2 Delicata squash
- ½ lemon
- 2 tablespoons coconut oil
- 4 tablespoons garlic oil

- ¾ tablespoons salt
- ¼ tablespoons black pepper
- 1/8 tablespoons paprika

DIRECTIONS

1. Preheat oven to 350 F
2. Remove seeds from the squash and cut in small pieces
3. Put strips into a baking dish and add garlic oil and spices over squash and mix squash
4. Add butter to pan and bake for 25-30 min
5. Stir squash and increase heat for another 20-25 minutes
6. Squeeze lemon over squash before they are done
7. Remove and serve!

Serves: **4**

Prep Time: **10** minutes

Cook Time: **15** minutes

Total Time: **25** minutes

INGREDIENTS

- 1 lb cauliflower head
- 3 tablespoons coconut oil
- ½ tablespoon horseradish mustard
- 1 tablespoons rosemary chopped
- 1 tablespoon salt
- ¼ tablespoon black pepper

DIRECTIONS

1. In a pot place the cauliflower and add water to boil until cauliflower is soft
2. Add the rest of the ingredients and blend until soft, cook for about 10-15 minutes
3. Remove and serve!

Serves: **6**

Prep Time: **5**   minutes

Cook Time: **15**   minutes

Total Time: **20**   minutes

INGREDIENTS

- 1 zucchini shredded
- 1 carrot shredded
- 2 eggs
- ¾ cup parmesan cheese
- ½ tablespoon salt
- 1/8 tablespoon black pepper
- 1/8 tablespoon red pepper
- ¼ cup coconut flour
- ½ tablespoon lemon juice
- garlic oil

DIRECTIONS

1. In a bowl combine all the ingredients
2. Move the mixture to a skillet over medium heat
3. Form 6 patties and fry on both sides

Serves: **4**

Prep Time: **10** minutes

Cook Time: **35** minutes

Total Time: **45** minutes

INGREDIENTS

- olive oil
- 1 large eggplant
- 1 medium zucchini
- 14 oz diced tomatoes
- 2 teaspoons paprika
- ¼ cup tomato sauce
- chopped basil
- salt

DIRECTIONS

1. In a pan add olive oil and cook over medium heat
2. Add eggplant and sauté for a couple of minutes
3. Add diced tomatoes, paprika, zucchini and tomato sauce and cook for 20-25 minutes
4. Stir in basil and season with salt

Serves: *4*

Prep Time: *10*   minutes

Cook Time: *35*   minutes

Total Time: *45*   minutes

INGREDIENTS

- 4 russet potatoes
- 1 cup water
- 1-2 tablespoons olive oil
- ¼ teaspoon salt

DIRECTIONS

1. Peel and chop the potatoes and place them into a saucepan over medium heat

2. Add water and cook for 20 minutes until potatoes are soft

3. Drain potatoes of water and add 1 tablespoon olive oil with ¼ of potato water

4. Mash the potatoes and mix with all the ingredients and with potato water also

5. Add more salt if needed and enjoy!

Serves: *4*

Prep Time: *15* minutes

Cook Time: *15* minutes

Total Time: *30* minutes

INGREDIENTS

- 1 celeriac root
- ½ cup chopped parsley
- 1 stalk celery
- ¼ cop pomegranate seeds
- ¼ cup almonds
- 1 teaspoon cumin seeds
- 2 tablespoons olive oil
- 1 tablespoon lemon juice
- salt

DIRECTIONS

1. In a food processor add cubed celeriac and blend until is very small
2. In a skillet toast cumin seeds over low heat and whisk with olive oil, salt and lemon juice

3. Add cumin seeds and stir
4. In another bowl mix celery, celeriac, parsley, almonds and pomegranate seeds and toss
5. Taste and adjust salt

ROASTED PADRONS

Serves: *4*

Prep Time: *5*   minutes

Cook Time: *10*   minutes

Total Time: *15*   minutes

INGREDIENTS

- Olive oil
- 1 pint padron peppers
- salt
- pepper

DIRECTIONS

1. Preheat a skillet over medium heat and add 1 teaspoon of olive oil

2. Add peppers and toss for 5-6 minutes

3. Sprinkle with pepper and salt, remove and serve

CUCUMBER BLUEBERRY SALSA

Serves: *4*

Prep Time: *5*   minutes

Cook Time: *10*   minutes

Total Time: *15*   minutes

INGREDIENTS

- ½ cucumber
- ½ pint blueberries
- 1 tablespoon chopped jalapeno
- 2 green onions
- ¼ fresh cilantro
- juice of 1 lime
- salt

DIRECTIONS

1. In a bowl combine all ingredients and stir
2. Adjust with salt and taste
3. Serve!

GREEN SALAD

Serves: 3
Prep Time: 5   minutes

Cook Time: 5   minutes

Total Time: 10   minutes

INGREDIENTS

- 6 leaf lettuce
- 2 teaspoons olive oil
- 1 teaspoon apple vinegar
- 1teaspoon lemon juice
- 1/8 teaspoon black pepper
- 1/8 teaspoon salt

DIRECTIONS

1. In a bowl chop the lettuce
2. Add the dressing ingredients in a jar with lid and pour the dressing over the lettuce and toss
3. Taste and adjust with salt

GARDEN HERB ZOODLES

Serves: *3*

Prep Time: *5*   minutes

Cook Time: *5*   minutes

Total Time: *10* minutes

INGREDIENTS

- 2 zucchini
- 1 teaspoon coconut oil
- 3 springs rosemary
- 3 springs fresh thyme
- 1 teaspoon garlic oil
- fresh basil

- salt

DIRECTIONS

1. Using a Spiralizer turn zucchini into zoodles(noodles)
2. In a saucepan mel coconut oil over low heat
3. Add thyme nad rosemary
4. Add zoodles and also garlic oil
5. Cook for 5 minutes and reduce heat to low
6. Season with salt and top with basil

ROSEMARY ROASTED POTATOES

Serves: *4*
Prep Time: *10*   minutes

Cook Time: *35*   minutes

Total Time: *45*   minutes

INGREDIENTS

- 6 red potatoes

- 2 tablespoons olive oil
- 3 tablespoons chopped rosemary
- salt

DIRECTIONS

1. Preheat oven to 400 F
2. On a baking sheet, place the red potatoes and drizzle with olive oil
3. Sprinkle with rosemary and stir
4. Sprinkle with salt and bake for 25-30 minutes
5. Remove from oven, let it cool and serve!

KALE CHIPS

Serves: **2**

Prep Time: **10** minutes

Cook Time: **55** minutes

Total Time: **65** minutes

INGREDIENTS

- 1 bunch kale
- 1 tablespoon olive oil
- 1 tablespoon yeast
- ¼ teaspoon salt
- ¼ teaspoon black pepper
- 1/8 teaspoon cayenne pepper

DIRECTIONS

1. Preheat oven to 200 F
2. Chop kale in medium small pieces
3. Place kale onto 2 parchment baking sheets
4. Drizzle with olive oil
5. In a bowl mix salt, pepper, yeast and cayenne pepper
6. Sprinkle the kale chips with mixture
7. Cook for 1 hour, remove from the oven and let cool

Serves: *4*

Prep Time: *30*   minutes

Cook Time: *35*   minutes

Total Time: *65*   minutes

INGREDIENTS

- 1 endive
- 7-ounce sockeye salmon
- 1 cup spinach
- 1 carrot
- 1 stalks celery
- 1 tablespoon curry powder
- 3 tablespoon mayonnaise
- 1 tablespoon olive oil
- ¼ cup lemon juice
- ¼ teaspoon black pepper
- ¼ teaspoon cayenne pepper
- ¼ cup chopped walnuts
- 4 tablespoons dried cranberries

DIRECTIONS

1. In a bowl combine spinach, carrot, celery, salmon, 1 teaspoon curry powder, lemon juice, olive oil, walnuts, cayenne and black pepper, cranberries
2. Taste and add salt if needed
3. On a plate prepare endive and scoop salmon salad into endive
4. Serve!

MEDITERRANEAN ROASTED VEGETABLES

Serves: *4*
Prep Time: *20*   minutes

Cook Time: *35*   minutes

Total Time: *55*   minutes

INGREDIENTS

- 1 eggplant
- 3 zucchini
- 2 red peppers
- 4 green onions

- 4 tablespoons olive oil
- 2 teaspoons coriander
- 1 teaspoon cumin
- 1 teaspoon turmeric
- ¼ teaspoon salt
- 1/8 teaspoons black pepper

DIRECTIONS

1. Preheat oven to 400 F
2. Chop the eggplant and red pepper and green onion in small pieces
3. Spread the vegetable on parchment baking sheets and drizzle with oil
4. In a bowl combine coriander, turmeric, salt and pepper and stir
5. Sprinkle the mixture over the vegetables
6. Cook for 20-25 minutes
7. When ready remove from the oven and let it cool

CHOC CHIP GRANOLA BARS

Serves: **2**

Prep Time: **10**   minutes

Cook Time: **30**   minutes

Total Time: **40**   minutes

INGREDIENTS

- 2 cups mixed nuts
- 2 cups shredded coconut
- 2 tablespoons almond flour
- ¼ cup cacao
- 1 tablespoon cinnamon
- ½ tablespoon salt
- ½ cup coconut oil
- ¼ cup almond butter
- ¼ cup honey
- 2 eggs
- 4 oz cacao

DIRECTIONS

1. Preheat oven to 325 F
2. Take a bowl and add nuts, almond flour, coconut, cacao, salt and cinnamon and mix well
3. Take another bowl and add coconut oil, honey vanilla and butter, melt them and stir until well mixed
4. In a bowl beat the eggs and stir them into the mixture, add the melted mixture to the rest of the ingredients
5. Spoon the mixture into a tin
6. Bake for 20-25 minutes

COCONUT PANCAKES

Serves: 2

Prep Time: *10*   minutes

Cook Time: *10*   minutes

Total Time: *20*   minutes

INGREDIENTS

- 1 banana

- 4 eggs
- 4 tablespoons almond flour
- 1 tablespoons baking powder
- 2-3 tablespoons butter
- 1 cup mixed berries, strawberries and raspberries
- 4 tablespoons coconut yoghurt

DIRECTIONS

1. In a bowl mix the eggs with the banana, almond flour, baking powder and the butter
2. Place a skillet over high heat and add 1 tablespoon of butter and then add the pancake mixture
3. Reduce the heat to low and let it cook, turn over and cook on the other side also
4. Remove from that pan and set aside to cool
5. Place the mixed fruits in a pan and cook on low heat, remove and top over the pancakes

Serves: 2

Prep Time: 10   minutes

Cook Time: 24   hours

Total Time: 24   hours and 10 minutes

INGREDIENTS

- 8 cups coconut milk
- 2 tablespoons honey
- yoghurt starter

DIRECTIONS

1. In a pan add the milk over medium heat
2. Add the yoghurt starter and the honey and stir them
3. Pour the mixture into a yoghurt make machine and leave it for 24 hours, once is ready remove and place it in the fridge

Serves: **4**

Prep Time: **5** minutes

Cook Time: **10** minutes

Total Time: **15** minutes

INGREDIENTS

- 1 banana
- 4 eggs
- 4 tablespoons almond flour
- 1 tablespoon baking powder
- 2-3 tablespoons butter

DIRECTIONS

1. Mix the eggs, banana, almond flour and the baking powder in a bowl
2. Place a skillet over high heat and add one tablespoon of butter and let it melt
3. Pour the mixture and reduce the heat, cook slowly and flip on each side for 5-10 minutes
4. Remove and set aside and let it cool

Serves: *4*

Prep Time: *5*   minutes

Cook Time: *30*   minutes

Total Time: *35*   minutes

INGREDIENTS

- 8 oz coconut milk
- 8 oz almond milk
- 3 tablespoons raw cocoa powder
- 2 tablespoons honey
- ½ cup raw cocoa butter
- ¼ cup raw cocoa powder
- ½ tablespoons stevia

DIRECTIONS

1. In a bowl mix coconut and almond milk and mix them, add boiling water and cacao powder and stir constantly. When the ingredients are well mixed add honey and continue to stir
2. Place the mixture into a ice cream machine

3. For chocolate chips take cacao butter and place it in a heat resistant bowl and microwave for 30 second – 1 minute, remove and add stevia and mix them

4. Pour the chocolate on a parchment paper and allow to cool

5. When the ice cream is done add the chocolate chips

MERINGUE TREE

Serves: **2**

Prep Time: **10** minutes

Cook Time: **120** minutes

Total Time: **130** minutes

INGREDIENTS

- 12 egg whites
- 2 cups glucose
- 2 tablespoons vanilla powder
- 6 cups coconut milk
- 1 tablespoon vanilla powder
- 4 cups strawberries

- 4 cups raspberries

DIRECTIONS

1. Preheat the oven to 225 F and take 4 baking sheets and cover them with baking paper, draw circles on the baking paper

2. In a bowl add the egg whites a mix with a hand mixer and add glucose and slowly mix them them, when fully incorporated add vanilla powder

3. Use the circles to divide the meringue mixture across the four tray, pace in the oven and bake for 60 minutes

4. When is ready stop the heat and let the meringues cool in the over for a couple of more minutes

5. In a bowl add coconut milk and add vanilla powder and mix them

6. When done take the largest circle on a cake tray and top with the whipped coconut, lay strawberry and raspberries over the top

CHOCOLATE COCONUT BITES

Serves: *2*

Prep Time: *90*   minutes

Cook Time: *30*   minutes

Total Time: *120*   minutes

INGREDIENTS

- 1 ½ cup shredded coconut
- ½ cup coconut milk
- 1 tablespoon coconut oil
- 1 tablespoon honey
- 1 cup raw cacao butter
- ½ cup cocoa powder
- ½ tablespoon stevia

DIRECTIONS

1. In a food processor add coconut oil, coconut oil and honey
2. Take a baking paper and some coconut mixture and roll into small balls, place in the freezer for 1 hour
3. In a heat resistant bowl add cacao butter and microwave for 1-2 minutes until the cacao butter has melted, add stevia in the cacao butter and mix

4. Pour the chocolate mixture over a baking paper
5. Return the bowl to the microwave for 1-2 minutes
6. Remove the coconut balls from the freezer and cover them with melted chocolate
7. Refrigerate for 5-10 minutes

STRAWBERRIES AND CREAM POPSICLES

Serves: *4*

Prep Time: *10*   minutes

Cook Time: *240*   minutes

Total Time: *250*   minutes

INGREDIENTS

- 2 cups strawberries
- 400 ml coconut milk

DIRECTIONS

1. In a blender add 1 cup of strawberries and mix well

2. In a bowl pour the coconut milk and add chopped strawberries

3. Pour the strawberry puree into the coconut mixture

4. Pour the strawberry coconut mixture into the molds and free for 60-90 minutes and a popsicle stick, every 60 minutes for next 3h check them to see if they are ready

STRAWBERRY SHORTBREAD COOKIE

Serves: *12*

Prep Time: *30* minutes

Cook Time: *10* minutes

Total Time: *40* minutes

INGREDIENTS

- 1 cup strawberries
- 1 tablespoon honey
- 2 tablespoons coconut flour
- 4 tablespoons butter
- 2 tablespoons honey
- 1 tablespoon vanilla

DIRECTIONS

1. Preheat oven to 325 F and line a baking sheet
2. In a bowl add coconut flour and butter and mix, add the vanilla powder and honey after that mix well
3. Take some mixture and roll into small balls and place on a baking sheet
4. Bake them for 5-10 minutes, when ready remove from the oven

PUDDDING WITH WARM CUSTARD

Serves: *4*

Prep Time: *30*   minutes

Cook Time: *30*   minutes

Total Time: *60*   minutes

INGREDIENTS

- 4 eggs
- 2 bananas
- 1 ½ cups almond meal

- 2 tablespoons honey
- 3 tablespoons coconut oil
- ½ tablespoon cinnamon
- ½ tablespoon nutmeg
- ½ tablespoon ground ginger
- ½ tablespoon mace
- ½ tablespoon baking powder
- ½ tablespoon baking soda
- 1 orange zest
- 4 egg yolks
- 2 cups almond milk
- 1 tablespoon vanilla
- 2 tablespoons honey

DIRECTIONS

1. Preheat the oven to 325 F, grease a 16 cup muffin pan with coconut oil
2. Mix bananas with eggs and add in a food processor, pour batter into the muffin pan and bake for 20 minutes and remove from the oven, let it cool for 5 minutes
3. For custard heat vanilla powder, honey and almond milk, in a separate bowl mix egg yolk
4. Pour almond milk over the yolk and continue to mix and them pour all the milk into in yolks
5. Cook the mixture in a heat proof bowl over low heath

Serves: *2*

Prep Time: *10*   minutes

Cook Time: *20*   minutes

Total Time: *30*   minutes

INGREDIENTS

- 4 eggs
- 2 tablespoons honey
- 3 tablespoons oil
- ½ cup coconut flour
- ¾ cup almond milk
- 1 tablespoon vanilla powder
- ½ tablespoon baking soda
- ½ tablespoon baking powder
- ¼ tablespoon salt
- 1 cup blueberries

DIRECTIONS

1. Preheat oven to 325 F
2. Take a 16 cup muffin pan and grease it with coconut oil

3. Mix honey, eggs and melted coconut oil and add them in a food processor

4. Add almond milk, baking soda, coconut flour, baking powder and salt, mix well

5. Spoon the batter into the muffin tins and bake for 20 minutes

6. Remove from the oven and let them cool for 5 minutes

7. Serve warm and store the remaining muffins

CHOCOLATE CARAMEL SLICE

Serves: 2

Prep Time: 30 minutes

Cook Time: 240 minutes

Total Time: 270 minutes

INGREDIENTS

BASE

- 2 cups almond meal
- ¾ cup coconut

- 80g butter
- 1 ½ tablespoon honey
- 1 tablespoon vanilla

CHOCOLATE TOPPING
- ½ cup coconut oil
- 1 cup cocoa powder
- 1 tablespoon stevia

CARAMEL
- 800 ml coconut milk
- ¼ cup honey
- 80g butter

DIRECTIONS

1. Preheat the oven to 325 F and line a brownie tin with a non-stick paper, combine desiccated coconut and almond meal in a bowl, melt honey and butter
2. Add vanilla and mix everything and press into the base of the tin, bake for 15 minutes
3. For caramel, take a saucepan and pour coconut milk, boil them and while boiling stir constantly
4. Reduce the heat and simmer, meanwhile add honey and cook for 30 minutes, add the butter to the mixture
5. Pour the mixture into the tin and bake for 15 minutes, remove from the oven and let it cook

6. **For chocolate topping combine all the ingredients, pour over the caramel and put everything in the fridge**

SUGAR FREE ORANGE AND MINT CHOCOLATES

Serves: **2**

Prep Time: **30** minutes

Cook Time: **10** minutes

Total Time: **40** minutes

INGREDIENTS

- 250 cacao butter
- 1 cup cacao powder
- ½ 1 tablespoon natural stevia
- mint oil
- orange oil

DIRECTIONS

1. **In a bowl chop the cacao butter and microwave for 1-2 minutes**

2. Sift in the stevia and cacao powder, pour the mixture onto a paper

3. Scrape the thickened chocolate off the baking paper and them return to a bowl, microwave for a couple of seconds

4. Divide the mixture, pour half in a bowl and add mint oil and stir into the first half and orange oil into the second bowl

5. Pour each mixture in a plastic bag

6. Pour one flavor into small chocolate molds, place the trays in the fridge for 10 minutes

7. Remove and serve!

HOT CROSS BUNS

Serves: 2

Prep Time: 20 minutes

Cook Time: 25 minutes

Total Time: 45 minutes

INGREDIENTS

- 4 eggs
- 1 banana

- 2 tablespoon honey
- 3 tablespoon coconut oil
- ½ cup almond meal
- 1 tablespoon mixed spice
- 1 tablespoon nutmeg
- 1 tablespoon cinnamon
- ½ tablespoon ginger
- zest from 1 orange
- zest from 1 lemon
- 1 tablespoon baking powder
- ½ tablespoon baking soda
- ½ cup almond milk

DIRECTIONS

1. Preheat the oven to 325 F
2. Grease a muffin tin with coconut oil
3. In a bowl place a banana and mash it, add honey, eggs and mix them. Add almond meal, coconut flour, zests, baking soda and baking powder and mix them
4. Pour the mixture into a 8 muffin holes for large buns
5. In another bowl mix 2-3 coconut flour and 1 cup almond milk and pour the mixture in a plastic bag
6. Place it in the oven for 20 minutes and remove when baked and let it cool a couple of minutes

Serves: 2

Prep Time: 30   minutes

Cook Time: 10   minutes

Total Time: 40   minutes

INGREDIENTS

- Coconut oil
- ¼ cup honey
- 1 cup raspberries
- 1 lemon
- 5 egg whites

DIRECTIONS

1. Preheat the oven to 400 F and wipe with coconut oil 6 ramekin dishes, also melt some honey
2. Juice a lemon and set aside
3. Blitz the raspberries in a blender until liquefy and set aside in a bowl
4. In another bowl add eggwhites and beat them, slowly drizzle in the honey while beating the eggs
5. Place the mixture in a spoonful of the meringue mixture into the raspberry mixture

6. Move the raspberry mixture into the meringue mixture

7. Spoon the meringue into ramekin dishes, bake for 10-15 minutes, remove and serve right after

Serves: *1*

Prep Time: *20*   minutes

Cook Time: *20*   minutes

Total Time: *40*   minutes

INGREDIENTS

- 250g cacao butter
- 1 cup cacao powder
- ½ powdered stevia
- 4 freeze dried strawberries

DIRECTIONS

1. Chop the cacao butter and place it in a silicone bowl and microwave for 1-2 minutes

2. Sift the cacao and stevia powders and then pour pour the mixture onto a baking paper

3. Scrape the chocolate off the baking paper, return to the bowl and heat in the microwave for a couple of more seconds

4. Pour the chocolate into small ice cube trays and leave room for the strawberries, sprinkle the strawberries over the top of the chocolate

5. Transfer the trays in the fridge for 10 minutes

6. Remove from ice cube trays and serve

SUMMER PINEAPPLE WITH COCONUT WHIP

Serves: *4*

Prep Time: *30*   minutes

Cook Time: *30*   minutes

Total Time: *60*   minutes

INGREDIENTS

- ½ 14 oz can coconut milk
- ½ tablespoon vanilla powder
- 2-3 tablespoons coconut oil

- 8 slice pineapple
- 1 orange zest
- 1 lime zest

DIRECTIONS

1. Preheat the over to 325 F
2. Heat the ghee in a bowl and zest the lemon
3. Add the zest in the bowl and also add 1 tablespoon of thyme leaves
4. Pat dry chicken and remove the skin from the meat and pull it away from the meat

COCO NUTTY BITES

Serves: **10**

Prep Time: **30**   minutes

Cook Time: **30**   minutes

Total Time: **60**   minutes

INGREDIENTS

- 1 tablespoon almond butter

- 1 tablespoon butter
- ¼ cup cacao powder
- ¼ cup coconut
- 1-2 tablespoons almond milk
- 1-2 tablespoons honey

DIRECTIONS

1. In a bowl mix the almond butter, honey, cacao powder and macadamia butter
2. Add 1 tablespoon of almond milk and mix, place the excess coconut and cacao powder on a separate plate
3. Scoop a spoonful of mixture onto one a spoon, shape it into a tight bite and use another spoon to leverage it off and place it in coconut and cacao powder
4. Set aside on a separate plate and repeat the process

Serves: **4**

Prep Time: **30** minutes

Cook Time: **30** minutes

Total Time: **60** minutes

INGREDIENTS

- 1 lime zest and juice
- 1 small fresh mint
- 2 cups water
- 4 drops liquid stevia

DIRECTIONS

1. In a bowl mix the juice and zest from the lime with mind and water, add stevia and pour the mixture into popsicle molds
2. Add sticks and place in the freezer for a couple of hours
3. Remove and enjoy!

Serves: *4*

Prep Time: *60* minutes

Cook Time: *60* minutes

Total Time: *120* minutes

INGREDIENTS

- 1 avocado
- 2 tablespoons cocoa powder
- 1 oz espresso
- 3 tablespoons organic honey
- 1 cup coconut milk

DIRECTIONS

1. In a food processor add cacao powder, avocado, honey and blend
2. Spoon into bowls and refrigerate for 1-2 hours and serve

Serves: **10**

Prep Time: **60** minutes

Cook Time: **120** minutes

Total Time: **180** minutes

INGREDIENTS

- 2 coconut
- 3 ½ tablespoons coconut butter
- 3 ½ coconut oil
- 1 tablespoon vanilla powder
- 4 drops liquid stevia
- ½ cup strawberries

DIRECTIONS

1. In a bowl add vanilla, stevia, melted coconut butter and mix
2. If necessary, add coconut oil to the mixture in case it is too dry and split the mixture into half
3. In a blender add strawberries and blend, stir through the strawberries into one serving of coconut
4. Add vanilla coconut in a loaf tin, pour over the strawberry coconut and pat down, refrigerat

Serves: **4**

Prep Time: **60** minutes

Cook Time: **60** minutes

Total Time: **120** minutes

INGREDIENTS

- 4 eggs
- 2 tablespoons almond meal
- 2 tablespoons coconut flour
- 1 tablespoon cocoa powder
- 4 drops liquid stevia
- ½ tablespoon vanilla powder
- ½ tablespoon baking powder
- 2 tablespoon cocoa nibs
- 1 cup strawberries
- 1 cup raspberries
- 2 tablespoons ghee
- ½ 14 oz can coconut milk

DIRECTIONS

1. Beat the eggs in a bowl, add coconut flour, cacao powder, almond flour, stevia, vanilla powder and baking powder and mix thoroughly
2. In a blender place berries and blend, set aside when ready
3. Heat a frying pan over high heat and melt the ghee, add 3-4 spoonsful of mixture in the pan and cook for 4-5 minutes on each side
4. Remove the tin of coconut milk from the fridge
5. Serve with piklets on a plate

CHOCOLATE BARK

Serves: 8
Prep Time: 120   minutes

Cook Time: 120   minutes

Total Time: 240   minutes

INGREDIENTS

- 1 cup cacao butter
- ½ cup cacao powder

- ½ tablespoon vanilla powder
- ¼ powdered stevia
- ¾ cup flaked coconut
- ½ cup hazelnuts
- 2 tablespoons pumpkin seeds

DIRECTIONS

1. Preheat the oven at 325 F, line a baking sheet with baking paper and place flaked coconut
2. In the oven place a tray for 5-10 minutes
3. When the coconut has toasted remove from the oven and set aside
4. Chop the cacao butter in even pieces and place them in the microwave for 1-2 minutes
5. In the melted cacao butter add stevia, vanilla powder and stir
6. Scrape the thickened chocolate off the baking paper, heat in the microwave for 10-15 seconds and stir
7. Pour the chocolate over a baking paper and sprinkle with coconut hazelnuts and pumpkin seeds. Place it in the fridge for 5-10 minutes
8. Once solid serve and store the remaining chocolate

THANK YOU FOR READING THIS BOOK!

Made in the USA
Las Vegas, NV
10 March 2022